The little college handbook

A FIRST GENERATION'S GUIDE TO GETTING IN AND STAYING IN

Melissa Mellott, M.Ed.

The Little College Handbook   Melissa Mellott

ISBN 0-9718345-2-0
Third Edition

Supported and Distributed by Advocacy Press · Santa Barbara, California ·
www.advocacypress.com

Comments on *The Little College Handbook...*

"*The Little College Handbook* is a practical, informative guide to the nuts and bolts of higher education -- **from choosing a major to figuring out financial aid.** Melissa Mellott shares her personal insights along with her expertise as a college admissions counselor to help readers understand the key steps involved with earning a college education."

-- Albert C. Yates, President, Colorado State University

"Being a first generation college student, I certainly would have benefited from having such a practical and helpful guide to the college environment. I would recommend the Handbook to all college bound students and their parents. **It provides invaluable and understandable answers to the many complex questions that heading to college can bring.**"

-- Sharyn Slavin Miller Ph.D., Assistant Vice President for Student Affairs, California Institute of Technology

"Melissa Mellott, speaking with true authenticity, grounded wisdom, and true dedication to the serious student, offers a practical navigational chart for the often murky waters of college application and education. **She recognizes the role of discipline, inspiration, and joy so vital to this life challenge.** The best predictor of success is often the skills and knowledge to get to the goal. Thank Melissa for showing the way and teaching the skills with such understanding and personal dedication."

-- Errol E. Erlandson MD, former Assistant Dean for Student Affairs, University of Michigan Medical School, Clinical Associate Professor of Surgery, University of Michigan, Ann Arbor, Michigan

"As the former Vice President of Cerritos College, I observed young people coming to college so unprepared. Melissa has walked the college path alone and learned how to   utilize resources, make contacts, and worked in college offices. As a result, she speaks with experience and shares it in such a way that she touches young people."

-- Fran Newman, Ed.D.Adjunct Professor, School of Education, Azusa Pacific University

"Thank you to Melissa Mellott for writing a book that is helpful for both college students and their parents.   We need as much information as we can get before taking the big step out of home and off to school. **Melissa is the voice of experience and her book will be an asset to students and parents alike."**

-- Susan Bridges, Mother of two college students, Montecito, California

"I have found *The Little College Handbook: Mapping Your College Dreams* to be a wonderful resource in working with prospective university students. **The author has done a terrific job in capturing the experience!"**

-- *Sara Axelson, Associate Vice President for Enrollment Management/Director of Admissions, University of Wyoming*

"In a down to earth and practical way and with an engaging and **authentically understanding style, Melissa Mellott will support you in opening the door to college!** She offers you her experience, practical insight, keen intuition, and gentle encouragement. The little details and the big picture are clearly contained in this rich little book. My own path would have been easier with this guidance, and a lot more joyous with her balanced approach. As a woman professional I applaud this gift and this accomplishment."

-- *Kate Ludeman Ph.D., Founder and President Worth Ethic Corporation, Author, Coach and Advisor to Fortune 100 companies, Santa Barbara, California*

"In *The Little College Handbook*, Melissa Mellott provides a terrific plan for using your college years to explore your interests so your **future career evolves as a natural extension** of your experience both inside and outside the classroom."

-- *Carol L. McClelland, Ph.D., Author of* **Changing Careers For Dummies**

"No you don't need a college degree to understand how to apply for admission to colleges and universities. **The Little College Handbook has taken the mystery out of a process that often seems overwhelming to students and parents.** In the little book, Melissa Mellott shares a lot of sensible guidance she has learned through personal experience as a college student and as an admission professional."

-- Mary Ontiveros, Executive Director of Admissions, Colorado State University

"*The Little College Handbook* is a valuable tool for any student or parent with questions about the college application process. It is **especially valuable to first generation college bound students.** Melissa writes in an "easy to read" and "easy to understand" style and **sprinkles the book with interesting personal experience and practical advice**."

-- Sue Bracco Gleason, Director, California Student Opportunity and Access Program, Santa Barbara, California Consortium

"This is important information for all high school students, especially those who think college is beyond their reach. **An educated society benefits us all, and this book takes us one step closer.**"

-- Judi A. Diaz-Bonacquisti, Director, Minority Engineering Program, Colorado School of Mines, Golden Colorado.

"*The Little College Handbook* is a great guide for students and parents that need help navigating the college admissions process. Melissa does a wonderful job of providing important college information in a **fun and easy-to-understand format**. I recommend the Handbook to any student feeling overwhelmed by the whole college process."

-- *Eric J. Carpio, Director of Admissions, Adams State College, Alamosa, Colorado*

"**Written in a style that students will enjoy reading**, *The Little College Handbook* gives practical advice and important, new details about planning and living the college experience."

-- *John T. McIntosh, Associate Superintendent, Ocean View School District, Oxnard, California*

Acknowledgements

After writing a book about college and the experiences of first generation students, it seems only appropriate to recognize the colleges I attended where I had the experiences that inspired me to write this book. Although a large university, *Colorado State University* had the "small town" character that made me feel more comfortable, especially my freshman year. I also had the pleasure of getting my first job in college admissions at CSU while I was a student; this experience allowed me to take another step out of my comfort zone and give presentations to large groups of prospective students!

Many thanks go to the faculty and staff at *Azusa Pacific University* where I earned my master's degree. My professors in the College Student Affairs program, staff and students challenged me to understand the ethics and heart that go into working in higher education. Sharyn Slavin-Miller, John Hoffman and Fran Newman were professors who stretched my mind and always cheered me on. The Office of Student Life at APU enabled me to work with students to establish the *Women's Resource Center*. Those students I worked with for two years are young people who shaped my heart and challenged my mind. The friends I met at APU, who share my passion working with college students, are a blessing and will also provide support in the advocacy of higher education for underrepresented students.

I am truly grateful to Joan Bowman at Advocacy Press for being an amazing mentor in this project. With her guidance, insight, and T.L.C. my book has benefited tremendously. I have gained a friend whose passion in her work makes her wisdom even more sincere. Being an educator herself and a former first generation student, Joan believes in the vision of my book; her support makes a significant difference.

Through Joan I met two people who waived their magic wands to enhance my book. Also a first generation student, Ronna Gordon not only used her editing skills but her experience and passion working with students to expand my book. As an educator, Ronna understood the purpose of the book, which was always evident in her notes and edits, carefully considering what students would understand and relate to. I am very appreciative of Ronna and her editing which improved the overall quality of the book.

I am also very thankful to Lora Tomova, the cover designer. An international student herself, she put her heart, soul and a lot of time and effort into creating a cover. Through her professionalism and creativity, I have seen a glimpse of how successful Lora's career will be in graphic design.

My friends and family continue to be my best cheerleaders. To one of my best friends, Ricky, I thank you from the bottom of my heart for your unconditional love and support through the ups and downs of this project. I am so thankful for you and your motivation in the production and management of my book. To my family, thank you to my parents for giving RJ and me the experience of growing up on a ranch in the little town of Del Norte, Colorado, complete with one stop light. Memories of those years gave me the insight and motivation I needed to write this book. To my brother RJ, the experiences you shared with me in your own high school career gave me the inspiration to write this book.

My personal experience as a college student, coupled with

my education and professional experiences with non-profit organizations such as Girls Inc. and College Summit, all gave me the resources and wisdom to better understand my own journey and that of other students. I recognize and appreciate the opportunities I have had to work with students from all walks of life. Each student inspired me with stories of courage, adversity and triumph. I thank all of the staff I worked with in various colleges and organizations, that continue to put their heart and soul into motivating and guiding young adults.

Table of Contents

Dedication

This book is dedicated to first generation college students, those first in their family to go to college and seek a higher degree.

"I took the one less traveled by, and that has made all the difference."
Robert Frost

Foreword
By J.B. Schramm

Today in America, there is an alarming chasm in the college enrollment of low-income populations relative to their more affluent counterparts. It's a grim reality. But the good news is that the problem is, to a large extent, fixable. And the place to start is by effectively disseminating information like the gold nuggets you'll find in this book.

The first person in a family to go to college ends poverty in a family line forever. Consider that college graduates will earn $1 million more than high school graduates over the course of their career,[1] and their children will be almost twice as likely to go to college themselves.[2] And the benefits of attending college extend beyond the family and into the community: college graduates contribute over $300,000 more in taxes over the course of their career, and the achievement of a higher education has been found to be the number one driver of urban economic growth.[3]

More than any other American institution, it's undeniable that college is now the gateway to full participation in civic life. At the same

---

[1] U.S. Census, 2001; U.S. Bureau of Labor, 1997.
[2] U.S. Census Data, various years; and U.S. Census, 2001; U.S. Bureau of Labor, 1997.
[3] "CEOs for the Cities: The Changing Dynamics of Urban America," Weissbourd, Robert, RW Ventures, and Berry, Christopher, Harvard University, October 7, 2003, p. iii.

time, though, low-income young people enroll in college at less than half the rate of their higher-income counterparts. Academic preparation surely accounts for part of this gap—but *only* part of it: low-income students in this country *who get As* enroll in college at the same rate as high-income students *who get Ds*[4]. Clearly, many students in this country must rely on a college transition system that doesn't work for them. As a result, we are losing out on masses of talent each year. In light of this, Melissa Mellott's *The Little College Handbook* is a valuable resource, packed with useful information that can help make real headway in putting *all* of America's talent on a path toward success.

Within an effective support system, first-generation students make powerful use of information. The organization I founded over ten years ago, College Summit, affects systemic change by pulling together critical players in a community to provide low-income schools with the tools, resources, and structure necessary to equip and empower their students to successfully navigate the college application and transition process.

Tired of seeing students "graduate" from the teen center to the street, several colleagues and I designed a system to help bright, low-income students who, with the right support and information during the

---

[4] *See* "The Intersection of Socioeconomic Status and College Participation," *Access Denied*, 1992-1993 BPS, College Board.

transition from high school to college, could propel their lives—and communities—in a positive direction. This important book has the very same goal.

Melissa Mellott knows this field as well as anyone. A first-generation college graduate herself, she has grappled first-hand with the inequities and challenges facing many students today. I commend her desire to make this information available in a digestible way for *all* of America's talented young people. This book will indeed help inspire generations of success.

J.B. Schramm
Founder and CEO,
College Summit, Inc.

Introduction

When I was 18 years old, I vividly remember attending a college information session. I sat in a room, surrounded by other anxious students and parents. The admissions counselor started the discussion by asking each of the students to introduce themselves by name, grade, and what their major would be in college. Some of the students were confident in their answers and seemed sure of their straight path to law school or medical school. Others seemed a little more hesitant or shy and didn't seem to have a clue as to what major they would choose. After each student's introduction, their parents would give that "I'm proud of you" smile. When it was my turn, I felt a little intimidated, especially after hearing the students who knew exactly what they wanted to do (at least they thought they did at the time). I gave my answer in a questioning tone – "My name is Melissa? I'm a senior? And I'm interested in occupational therapy?" Whew! I was glad that was over! I did not like being put on the spot and at that point I really couldn't imagine getting through four years of college.

After introductions, the admissions counselor discussed application requirements, academics, financial aid, and scholarships. In a 30 minute presentation, I heard the words majors, minors, credits, prerequisites, grants, unsubsidized loans, work-study, registration, undergraduate, graduate, bachelor's master's – it was like a word search in my brain and I had no idea what the meaning of these terms were. This college lingo was completely foreign to me. My brain was on information overload. I remember one parent asking, "What's the freshman retention rate?" What did that mean and why was it important? And how would I ever get through this?

If your parents did not earn a college degree, you are considered a first generation college student. The college application process is confusing for any student and parent, but for a first generation college student, it was (and is) overwhelming. So much so, that in my case, it made me want to forget about college altogether. As a junior or senior in high school, have you experienced this situation? The preparation for college and the transition from high school to college can be very intimidating.

In my parents' generation, going to college was not

considered to be as important as it is today. For Generation X, a college education was strongly encouraged. For the new generation, sometimes called the Millennials or Generation Y, it's almost a necessity. I have heard other educators say that today's bachelor's degree is like yesterday's high school diploma. Students today are not only encouraged to get that bachelor's, but to go beyond that, earning a master's or PhD to be competitive in the job market.

My parents quit high school and entered the job market right away. They pursued their dream of starting a family and living the quiet ranch life. If your parents did not go through the experience of applying to or attending college, you may find yourself without a mentor or advisor as you begin the process and this can be more than a little scary.

Helen Keller once said, "Life is a succession of lessons which must be lived to be understood." We all have life lessons, some smaller than others. Nevertheless, we still learn from our experiences. Being a first generation college student has been a life lesson for me. Because of my experiences, I can truly relate to students and their families preparing for college. I have attempted to put together a reference for these students in particular, but also for all prospective college applicants. Maybe this little book will help put the process into perspective and calm the panic that often comes when the reality of high school's end approaches! It is a tool for parents and students who are preparing to go to college or those students who are still trying to figure out the whole idea of "college." You will find easy steps, tips, vocabulary and personal stories. I hope this little college book gives you the basic knowledge to succeed in the transition from high school to college, college to career and everything in-between.

Chapter One

Where Are You in the College Process?

Topics Covered:

- **How this handbook will help you**
- **A short note to freshmen in high school**

Maybe you are a senior in high school – finally! And everybody – your friends, parents, even teachers are asking you "Where are you going to college?" or "What are you going to major in?" There is so much to consider; the questions below are probably just the start of what's going through your mind as you think about college:

> ➤ Where should I apply?
> ➤ How do I apply?
> ➤ When should I apply?
> ➤ When should I visit college campuses?
> ➤ Should I start at a community college and then transfer to a four-year college?
> ➤ Can I afford college and how exactly does the financial aid process work?
> ➤ Where/when/how can I research scholarships?
> ➤ What should I major in?

Or maybe you are a first generation college student – the first in your family to go to college and you need to know the basics. So you may be asking the above questions, but in more detail. You may be asking questions such as:

> ➤ What's the difference between a major and minor?
> ➤ How is an associate's degree different from a bachelor's degree?
> ➤ How does financial aid work and what is a grant, educational

loan, or work-study?

➢ Can I really afford college?

Maybe you are a freshman just starting college and you're still not sure what you want to major in and how that will impact future jobs and careers. It seems everyone around you has a major and a set path, but you're in limbo and you don't know where to go.

It's quite possible you have picked a major, but wonder what else you can do while you're in college to create a strong resume for future employers. You want to know about internships and job prospects while in college.

You may be a parent looking for guidance. You want to be familiar with the college process so that you can help your son or daughter through the transition from high school to college. The questions you may be asking include:

➢ When should we plan on visiting college campuses?

➢ What is my part in financial aid?

➢ What can/should I do to help my son or daughter apply to college?

A Short Note for Freshmen in High School

You may be wondering what you can do now to prepare for college. Here are a few things to think about.

It's never too early to start thinking about college – sort of…it's a good idea to starting thinking about your goals and talking with your family about "what you want to be when you grow up." However, don't put too much pressure on yourself so early in the game. By the time you're ready to go to college, you could already be burned out! Colleges *will* look at your grades, but don't overwhelm yourself with the details just yet.

During your freshman and sophomore years of high school, meet with your counselor to discuss selecting classes. Consider including your parents in these meetings or just talking with them at home.

If you haven't already done so, get involved in an extracurricular activity, something you really enjoy. Try to stay involved with that organization until your senior year. College admissions counselors like to see that a student is involved in something other than academics, such as sports, clubs, the arts, and community service. How does this help your chances of being accepted into college? It makes a student more well-rounded – a key term you will start hearing more often. For example, a leadership position in an organization or sports club would balance your application and make you a stronger candidate. Of course being the captain of the football team is not going to make up for the failing grade you received in algebra, but you get the idea.

But don't think joining a ton of clubs is the ticket into college – it's not! Generally, college admissions counselors would rather see a student who has been dedicated to the *same* one or two organizations throughout their high school years. Plus you don't want to sacrifice your grades – grades are still the key factor in college admission decisions.

A job can also be a good extracurricular activity. Although it's helpful to learn to handle money, as well as to manage time responsibly, I would caution against spending too much time in the work place. Research shows that a part-time job in high school is more harmful than helpful. The opposite is true of a part-time job in college, which will be discussed in chapter four. Of course, family circumstances may put you in a position where you have to work.

The key is balance. You'll read the words "balanced" and "well-rounded" throughout this book because that is exactly what admissions counselors and employers want to see on an application or resume. Colleges want to admit students who are bright and involved. They want to add diversity to their campus. Admissions officers are looking for first generation college students, ethnic minorities, females pursuing science or engineering, international students, artists and musicians. Think about what you may do during high school to add diversity to your own experience.

Chapter Two

**Visiting College Campuses
Not Just Pretty Pictures**

Topics Covered:

- **What is the ideal time to visit college campuses?**
- **What questions should you ask the tour guide or admissions representative?**

Students start their college search by researching maybe on the internet, attending college fairs or reading a viewbook they got from their high school counselor's office. Based on what they learn, they apply to the colleges that fit their personal and academic needs.

A critical step is sometimes forgotten in the process of researching colleges. Students often make a decision as to where they are going to college based on what they've read or heard about a particular school or the appealing photographs in the viewbook. What's wrong with this picture? The research is not complete. The next step should be visiting the college campus. Students should plan on visiting the college they are interested in to ask questions about the college and to see if it's a good "fit" for them.

Think about it for just a moment. You will probably be living in that particular college environment for at least four years. When you arrive on the campus, ask yourself if you feel the students, staff and professors are helpful and friendly. Is the community welcoming? What about the natural surroundings – is the climate an appealing environment for your interests such as hiking, biking, skiing, surfing?

All of these factors play a big part in the success of your college experience. Indeed, you want to pick a college with solid academics, especially for your area of study, but can you make it a *home*? If you are not happy in your living environment, you may not flourish in the college experience.

Websites for College Research

www.usnews.com	"Best Colleges" Ranking
www.petersons.com	Admissions and financial aid
www.nacac.com	Admissions information

When to Visit

The ideal time to start visiting colleges is the end of your junior year in high school, throughout the summer, and into your senior year. Don't wait until the summer before you are to start college that fall!

I worked with a student who applied to a reputable college, but didn't visit the campus until the orientation program (which is usually the summer before classes start). The student arrived on campus and was disappointed by what he thought would be a perfect fit. Luckily, at the last minute, there was still space at his second choice college, but registering for classes and getting a dorm room was difficult.

During your senior year, you are under time pressure to make a decision as to what school you want to attend. Visiting a campus and either falling in love with it or not, may eliminate some of your choices.

There are many factors to take into consideration when selecting a college: public versus private, academics, cost, size, and location. To find out more about the college, I have put together a list of questions you should ask a college representative. You may need to refer to the glossary in the back of the book to find definitions of what is often confusing college lingo.

<u>Questions to ask the college representative or tour guide</u>

Enrollment Questions

1. What is the total enrollment of the college (how many students attend)? What percentages are graduate students and undergraduates?

2. What is the size of the incoming freshman class? What percentage is in-state and out-of-state?

Diversity Questions

1. What is the percentage of ethnic minorities on campus?

2. What is the percentage of international students on campus?

3. Do you have support services for women pursuing science or engineering fields?

4. Do you have advocacy offices for ethnic minority and first generation college students?

5. Do you have support services for students with disabilities?

Admission Questions

1. How many applications did the college receive for incoming freshman in the past year?

2. What is the acceptance rate of the freshmen who apply?

3. Do you give additional consideration for students with certain hardships? (Learning disabled, first generation college students, other)

4. Do you have a rolling admission process?

5. When do you encourage freshman to apply and what is the deadline date?

6. What is the geographical breakdown of the freshman class?

Academics

1. What is the student to faculty ratio?

2. What is the average class size?

3. Is there an honors program? What are the requirements and deadlines for acceptance and are honors classes typically smaller?

4. What percentages of professors have a Ph.D.?

5. Are any of your majors nationally ranked?

6. What percentage of students graduate in four years?

7. What is the freshman retention rate?

Housing

1. Are freshmen required to live on campus?

2. What percentages of students move off campus the second year?

3. What housing accommodations or resources do students

have for off-campus housing?

4. Is there a dorm room I may look at?

Transportation

1. Are students allowed to have cars?

2. What is the cost of parking permits?

3. What is the main mode of transportation on campus?

4. Is public transportation available?

5. What transportation is available to get to an airport and how far is the campus from an airport and a major city?

Medical

1. Is there a health clinic on campus? Is it staffed with a medical doctor?

2. Is health insurance available and if so, what is the cost?

3. What other health services are available (dental, physical therapy, pharmacy, etc.)?

Safety

1. Is the campus well-lit?

2. What type of safety programs does the campus have?

3. What is the crime rate on campus?*

*Campuses are required to provide their campus crime statistics. This report can usually be found on each institution's website.

Social and Extracurricular

1. How many clubs and organizations?

2. Club and intramural sports?

3. NCAA Athletics?

4. Do students typically leave campus on the weekends? In other words, is the campus considered a "suitcase" campus?

5. What percentage of the campus is Greek (fraternities and sororities)?

6. What types of cultural activities and internship opportunities are available in the local community?

Can you think of other questions that you should ask the tour guide or admission representative?   Think about the ideal college environment for your needs – what questions come to mind? Use the *Notes* page at the back of the book to make a list of your own questions.

Chapter Three

Creating a Balanced College Application

Topics Covered:

- **What does an admissions counselor look for on the transcript?**
- **What if your ACT or SAT scores aren't as high as you had hoped?**
- **What makes your essay stand out to an admission counselor?**

You want to make the process of applying to college as painless as possible. It can be simple, really. The first thing you need to find out is the earliest date that you may apply. Some colleges allow you to apply at the end of your junior year, others not until the beginning of your senior year. Keep in mind the earlier you apply, the less stressed you will be. Applying early will also allow valuable time for college visits, scholarship searches and just enjoying your last year of high school. To make this process easier to understand, I am going to tell you what documents you will need to apply and what admissions counselors look for in each document you will be providing in the application packet.

Another important factor that I want you to consider is where to apply. First, this chapter will share with you how to create a solid, balanced application. However, if you apply to a college and are not admitted, don't get discouraged! You may have applied to a college that you have always dreamed of attending, but hopefully, you have also applied to your second and third choice colleges. If your cumulative GPA is a 3.0, then you shouldn't apply to all Ivy League schools, but also to some more realistic choices whose admission requirements fit your profile. If you don't get into your dream school, there's always the option of transferring later, which you can read about in chapter eleven.

As you read in the previous chapter, visiting college campuses will give you a good perspective of what a college is all about academically and socially and whether or not it is a good fit for you. When you get to the point of filling out your college applications, you want to consider all you learned on the college tours, but you should also consider other variables. Here are some of the main factors and questions you should consider when applying to and choosing a college:

- Do you meet the admissions requirements?
- Do you want to attend a large university or a small college?
- Do you want to attend a college in the city or in a smaller town?
- How far away do you want to be from home?
- Do you want to stay in your home state or go out of state?

Official High School Transcripts

The most substantial document you will need to submit is your high school transcript, which will list the classes you have taken throughout high school, as well as your cumulative grade point average (GPA). "Cumulative" is the operative term – this means your earned grades since you started high school, freshman through senior year.

The first thing admissions counselors will check are your grades. Because the cumulative GPA is being considered, it's important that you do well throughout high school, *not just your junior and senior year.*

Another important factor is the variety and type of classes that you have taken throughout high school. College admissions counselors like to see that you have taken advanced placement, international baccalaureate (IB), college prep and/or honors classes. These types of courses may help you score higher on the ACT and/or SAT or SATII and they will also better prepare you for college academics. Also, you can often get college credit for AP classes taken in high school.

A strong academic schedule is a way to create balance with your grades. As an admissions counselor, I reviewed hundreds of applications. I considered a student to be a stronger candidate for admission if their schedule included AP Calculus or Honors English instead of Home Economics or Study Hall, for example.

Finally, admissions counselors look at trends in your grades. *Consistency* in your grades throughout high school is a *positive* trend if your grades remained average to above average. Maybe you're a student who started out with lower grades your freshman year as you were adjusting to the new pressures of high school, but steadily your grades got better. This is considered an *upward* trend, which is also *positive* in the eyes of an admissions counselor. On the other hand, a *downward* trend is the opposite – when your grades have declined; this is not a good scenario and makes the admission counselor wonder about your potential. If this is your situation, you may want to address it in your application essay. But, we'll talk more about that later.

So, as you can tell, the transcript is a key piece of your application. You will need to submit official high school transcripts to every college to which you apply. Before you send those applications, you should ask the following questions:

1. Does the college require a minimum grade point average? If

so, what is it?

2. What is the average grade point average, or middle fiftieth percentile GPA of the typical entering freshman?

3. What are the high school course requirements – how many years of English, math, natural science, social science and foreign language are needed?

By asking these questions you will know whether you're considered competitive enough to apply to that college. If you are not competitive enough for admission to the college of your choice, don't lose hope. Chapter eleven discusses the option of starting at a community college and transferring to a four-year school. Also, remember to be open-minded about which schools you apply to; there are so many fabulous schools out there, not just those with famous names.

Standardized Tests: ACT, SAT, SATII

Most four-year colleges require an ACT or SAT score.

However, these days, most colleges do not prefer one over the other. Colleges also require the SAT II. So the questions to ask are:

1. Which test does the college require?
2. What is the minimum test score to get into the college, or what is the average and/or middle fifty percentile score of students who are accepted?

High school and college counselors usually encourage students to take either test twice. Most colleges will consider combination scores. This means that if a student takes the test more than once, the college will take the highest sub-sections from each test to create a higher composite score. Students should plan on taking the test for the first time at the end of their junior year.

Many of the students I work with get discouraged because they do not score high on the test. It may be because they have "test anxiety" or, a learning disability; perhaps the testing conditions were not ideal. Whatever the reason, know that you are not alone if you are not a good test taker. Keep in mind the test score is only a piece of your application. Also, in my experience working with students and seeing them succeed in college, these tests are not always a good predictor of success. In fact, I got a 19 on my ACT, which was just below average at the time I took it. I look back on my achievements and my success in graduate school and realize the low score on my ACT had no impact on my accomplishments. All of the authors, business owners, and other very successful people I have worked with or interviewed, could not even remember their test score!

My advice to you is to study for the test by taking a prep class or using a computer program. If you can afford a couple of sessions with a private tutor to, say, brush up on some rusty math skills, which would be very helpful. But using a CD-Rom or test prep book on your own will also work if you have the discipline and motivation to use them regularly. Why not factor in a few half-hour sessions into your schedule when you sit down with your test prep material and review?

Study, take the test at least twice, and then know you did your best. Then forget about it! Keep in mind that these tests are very limited in what they are measuring – math, science, English and reading. Areas that you may excel in such as art, music, computers, business, and many other subjects are not even measured.

To learn more about each of these tests, talk with your high school counselor about details regarding the test and dates the tests are offered. You may also visit these websites for more information

ACT   *www.act.org*
SAT   *www.collegeboard.org*

<u>Personal Essay</u>

How do you write an impressive essay? There are books written on this subject alone! Here are a few points you should keep in mind when writing the personal essay.

First, ask the college admissions counselor for the topic of the essay. Chances are there is not a specific topic; the student may write about whatever he or she chooses. This puts a little pressure on the student by forcing some creativity – at least that's what the admissions counselor hopes.

I know from experience that admissions counselors read hundreds of essays a year. They look for essays that are unique and creative. Also, since many colleges do not have personal interviews, the essay will often act as the personal interview. Treat it as such. Submitting an essay that tells your individual story or explains why you would be successful at their campus makes your application profile more appealing. I've read essays that truly caught my attention, essays that I was anxious to share with the other counselors. These types of essays go beyond saying "I want to go to college to get a better job." They are often stories of tragedy, triumph, or traveling and use writing techniques which make them intriguing. Show your personality through your writing. Remember, the admissions counselor is often someone not much older than you; perhaps a recent college graduate, and he or she has a pile of essays to go through. Try to imagine him or her with stacks of applications to read and lots of coffee to keep them awake! Make your essay one that grabs their attention. If you have a story to tell about overcoming an obstacle or surviving a personal setback, dig deep inside yourself and write about it.

Also, keep in mind that if you have a downward trend in your grades and there is a good reason for it (extenuating circumstances), then consider addressing that in your essay. Admissions counselors *do* take this into consideration and *may* give additional consideration to a student who has faced adversity.

The personal essay is yet another way to create balance in your application packet. Maybe your grades and/or test scores are on the lower end of the scale. If you submit a stellar essay that shows potential or explains why you would be successful at that particular college, or how you would add diversity to the campus, that may give your application just the boost it needs to stand above the rest.

I've seen applications that are borderline acceptances, but have essays which support the decision to admit the student. These essays were well-written and pique my interest enough so that I didn't want to quickly skim through it. Rather, I read it and in the end felt like I knew the applicant on a more personal level. The essays that get the attention of admissions counselors are those that tell a story about how a specific person, event, or experience was influential.   When you write about these experiences, give vivid details, not cliché statements, which are unoriginal and dull to the admissions counselor who is reading it.

Another tip and one that may seem obvious: check your spelling and make sure you use the correct name of the institution to which you are applying all through the essay. You wouldn't believe how often, in the age of word processors, this gets overlooked. Even with spell check on your computer, proofreading is never unnecessary.

The personal essay is an important aspect of the application and is not to be taken lightly. You should spend some quality time reflecting on what you want to write about and what you would like to convey to the admissions counselor who will be reading your essay.

Letters of Recommendation

Letters of recommendation can sometimes have the same positive effect as an essay. So now the question is, whom can you ask to write praises about you? Most colleges prefer letters from someone in an academic setting, such as a counselor or teacher (versus a coach or employer). I would encourage you to request the letters early in your senior year, as teachers and counselors are bombarded with these requests from all of their students close to application deadlines. Respect their time and they will greatly appreciate it. Remember to include a stamped, addressed envelope as well as a cover letter thanking the person for writing on your behalf and including the date that it is due.

I have read letters that were helpful to the student, in which a teacher pointed out specific projects and examples of leadership and abilities. On the other hand, I have seen letters that may have been signed by an "important" person, but that were not helpful to the student's application because of the lack of personal commentary.

Putting the Pieces Together

If working on your application online, it's often helpful to first print out a hard copy, work from that, then transfer the information to the electronic application. If you submit a paper copy through the mail, remember to make copies of everything you send, and ask the Post Office for a "proof of mailing." This is inexpensive and DOES NOT REQUIRE A SIGNATURE ON THE OTHER END like a certified or registered letter, which you should absolutely NOT do! With a proof of mailing though, if your material gets lost, you may have some recourse. Also, make sure you hear back from the colleges, whether through email or post card that they received all the necessary application material.

Once you have finished submitting your complete applications, the hard part is over. I hope you have noticed the recurring theme in this section of the book: balance. There are a lot of details that make up the first big step into the college world. Most importantly, don't shy away from asking admissions counselors questions, and try to apply early to maximize your chances of getting into your first choice school!

Good luck with this first leap into your new chapter, and may you get into the college where you will best flourish academically and personally.

Admissions Decisions

You have put time and effort into presenting the best application possible; now it's up to the admissions counselors to make a decision. There are many details that go into the decision-making process. Admissions counselors are checking class schedules and trends in grades, reading essays and letters of recommendation; they are looking for reasons to admit you. Each college has different requirements. Some may require an interview and some may request first semester senior grades (usually counselors will do this if they see a slight downward trend; they want to make sure the trend is not continuing). Each application is unique, often requiring detailed attention to gain perspective on whether or not the student would be successful at that particular college. Generally speaking, there are three decisions which can be made:

Admit – Good job! Your hard work paid off!

Refuse/Deny – Do not get discouraged if you get a denial of admission letter.   Admissions counselors have made this decision because they did not want to set you up for failure if you did not meet the admission requirements of the college.   Read chapter eleven, which discusses the option of starting at a community college and then transferring to a four-year college.   The other option is applying to a college that better suites your academic profile.

Wait List – A student is usually wait listed if they do not meet the admissions requirements, but they show potential in areas of their application.   Depending upon how many spots are available, a student will usually know whether or not they are pulled off the wait list in mid-late spring, although it's not unheard of to even find out in summer.

<u>Confirming your Admission</u>

First the ball is in your court as you hustle to apply to colleges, then the admissions counselors take control as they mull over applications and make decisions.   Now you have a decision to make: you will need to *confirm* to one or more of the schools to which you were accepted.

Confirming your admission saves your spot in the freshman class. The national confirmation date is May 1, but it is to your benefit to confirm sooner. Often, housing assignments and priority registration for classes depends upon your prompt confirmation.

Chapter Four

Financial Aid
College is an Investment

Topics Covered:

- **Defining & understanding financial aid terms**
- **How does financial aid work?**
- **When to apply and who should apply?**
- **Financial aid timeline**

Before you cringe at the thought of reading about the process of financial aid and skipping to the next chapter, let me assure you this chapter actually will help you understand financial aid.

The reality is, most of us do not have enough money saved to go to college. But there's good news – everyone can afford to go to college! Some students (and parents) write off going to college because they think they cannot afford it. That is exactly what financial aid is for, to help students pay for college.

I will be honest with you; the process is confusing. I think a person needs to actually go through the process of applying for financial aid to truly understand it – remember what Helen Keller said about life lessons? "Life is a succession of lessons which must be lived to be understood." Going through the financial aid process was another lesson for me. As a first generation college student, it was even more difficult because my parents were as mind-boggled as I was – this is confusing stuff! I am going to share my life lesson with you so that you will understand how you can afford college.

I think the best way to explain financial aid is to first and foremost explain the terms. Yes indeed, college lingo again, but this time it's financial aid, which can be quite intimidating to parents and students.

Let's start with the basics.

Financial Aid Terms

Loans – Most of us are familiar with loans, but education loans are different and better than the typical bank loan. Okay, we know that a loan is money that must be paid back, but for the most part, education loans do not need to be repaid until the student graduates from college. There is a grace period of six months after you graduate, giving you time to get a job.

For the most part, loans will not accumulate interest until after the student has graduated from college. When you do graduate, the interest rate will vary, but it is usually fairly low, and will not exceed 8.25%. As a student you may or may not understand the importance of interest rates. Nevertheless, parents can understand low versus high interest rates.

Many students do not want to take out loans because of the debt they will have later, but let's face it – borrowing money for college is a fact of life for most of us and yes, you will have some debt and you will have to repay the loan.

However, because of the college degree you will have earned, you will be able to get a job with a better income than those without a degree. Statistics show the more schooling you have (bachelor's, master's, and doctorate), the more money you will make in your career. You have heard it before, but I will say it again – you have to spend money to make money and your education is an investment of a lifetime, something that no one can ever take from you!

Here are three definitions associated with loans you should familiarize yourself with:

PLUS Loans – Parent Loans for Undergraduate Students (PLUS) loans are taken out by the parents rather than the student and usually interest starts accumulating shortly after the loan has been disbursed. In other words, parents are required to start monthly repayment soon after the money is borrowed.

Subsidized Loans – The student does not have to pay interest on the loan while in school or during the grace period of six months after graduation.

Unsubsidized Loans – Interest accrues on the loan while the student is in school.

Grants – Grants are free money – that's right, grants are like gifts from the government. This is money the government gives you for your education that you never have to pay back. Grants are usually set aside for low-income families. So how does the government decide who gets the free money? Eligibility depends on the financial situation of the family, which will also be covered in this chapter.

Work-Study – Work-study is simply having a job on campus while you're in school. Before you panic and think, "How can I study and work at the same time and still get good grades?" Let me explain the benefits of work-study and how it actually does work for you, not against you.

Any student can get a job on campus working in the library or cafeteria, but here's a clue – work where you can get quality experience. For clarity, let's look at an example: you are in college studying journalism because you want to be a broadcaster. How about working at the college television station, radio station or newspaper? This is not only going to give you money in college, it's providing great experience on your resume (employers love that!), and great references.

Another tip – take initiative. Many students wait until a list of jobs is posted in the financial aid office – don't wait! If there's a place on campus you would like to work, call that office, stop by and let them know of your interest in working there. Do this the summer before you start classes.

Let's say, for example, you are a biology major, planning to go to medical school. Go to the health center and ask about work-study jobs. Or maybe you are a business student. Then visit the business department and ask about being a research assistant. Are you really good at math or English? Go to the tutoring center and ask about jobs.

Are you getting the idea? Employers love to see students who not only have a degree, but who also get job experience while they are in college. As an employer, what would be more attractive to you – someone who has straight A's and no job-related experience or an average student who has worked as a tour guide and had public speaking experience while they were in college? These early career experiences will give you a leg up on the employment ladder after graduation.

Think about your interests, strengths, or areas you would like to learn more about – use the *Notes* page to write down a list of places on campus that you may like to work.

What is Financial Aid and how does it work?

When discussing financial aid, I am referring to the *Free Application for Federal Student Aid*, or FAFSA. The FAFSA is the general financial aid application that students and parents must fill out in order to be considered for the money mentioned in the terms before – loans, grants, and work-study. Anyone can apply for financial aid through the FAFSA and it's a general application for all colleges and universities in the United States.

So how does a student get the money? The money from the FAFSA comes from the government (U.S. Department of Education) and a formula is used to determine how much money your parents are expected to contribute to your college education. Whatever portion the parents cannot pay, the FAFAS (or government) attempts to make up with loans, grants, and work-study.

Okay, so that was a mouthful and you are probably a little confused. Let's take the process piece by piece. You and your parents need to fill out the FAFSA, and many financial questions are asked. There are questions about such things as: assets, savings, income, number of children in family and number of children in college.

By asking these questions the government is figuring out what they call the "*Expected Family Contribution*", which is how much mom and dad can pay for your college expenses. Keep in mind this formula (EFC) looks at the whole picture of the family financial situation. The lower the EFC, the better chances you have of getting loans, grants and work-study.

Parents, I know what you're thinking: "So my children may not qualify for any money because I make a good income." This is not entirely the case. Remember the EFC formula is looking at the *whole* picture; you may indeed be making a good salary, but what about the other circumstances? If you have four children and two are already in college, then your higher salary doesn't mean as much as it would in a family with two children with none in college.

So again, the concept of balance comes to mind. Here's another factor to keep in mind: we (students and parents) are dealing with the government, so your idea of what you may contribute and the government's idea are sometimes conflicting. At the same time, financial aid is still helpful to most families. You may still be a little confused or even frustrated at this point, so let's look at a scenario of a family applying for financial aid.

For simplicity, let's take a very general example. Imagine an average size family of four, two parents/guardians and two children. The combined income of the parents is **$50,000** a year; there are a few assets, some debt and a little savings. After filling out the FAFSA and sending it into the government, the results are sent back to you stating the EFC is **$3,000** a year.

Okay, let's slow down a little, what does this mean? An EFC of **$3,000** means that's what the government thinks the parents/guardians can/should provide that year for college. However, the cost of the college is **$10,000** a year so that's a difference of **$7,000** a year – and that difference is made up in loans, grants and work-study. Some families may have an EFC of **$9,000** a year and may not qualify for any money.

On the other hand, I have worked with families whose EFC is $0 meaning the parents could not pay anything and therefore the student is completely funded through the FAFSA. This was my own case in college and is exactly the reason that I understand this frustrating and confusing process.

So then you may ask yourself, "Do I have a better chance of getting more money if I come from a single parent family?" And the answer is, quite possibly, yes, because there is only one income being considered, unless of course the one parent is making a high salary based on the EFC.

EFC Formula:

College Costs
(Tuition, fees, housing, books, transportation, personal expenses)

- **Your Expected Family Contribution**
(How much you and your parents are expected to pay for college)

= **Your Financial Need**

Visit College Board's website at **www.collegeboard.org** to calculate a practice Expected Family Contribution.

I know, I know, financial aid is a boring subject, but you are almost there, just a few more hints about financial aid. **First, know the FAFSA priority date of all of the colleges to which you apply.** Your FAFSA should be filed in the winter of your senior year. The longer you wait after the priority date, the less chance you have of getting a better financial aid package.

<u>When to Apply</u>

You will be able to get a FAFSA the first semester of your senior year. You may find a FAFSA at your high school counseling offices, and college admissions and financial aid offices. Although you and your parents may read through it, the FAFSA may not be filled out until after January 1st of your senior year. (The tax information from the past year will be needed and obviously cannot be obtained until the year is completely over and tax information is available after taxes are filed.) Parents, this is important to remember because as much as we loathe tax season and put off thinking abut it until the last minute, if you have a child who is entering college, taxes should be filed as soon as possible after the first of the year. As mentioned before, be aware of the priority dates of each college in order to have the FAFSA filled out in time.

A couple of tips: First, proofread your answers on the FAFSA; make sure your application is complete, accurate, and *signed*.

Second, keep copies of your tax information and the FAFSA for your records and verification.

<u>Who should apply for financial aid and why?</u>

Everyone should apply for financial aid and fill out the FAFSA, – even if you don't think you'll qualify. Here's why:

1. It's a free application and you won't lose any money by doing so.
2. It will take less than two hours of your time, especially if you file online.
3. Some scholarship committees require you to fill out the FAFSA, just to be considered for their scholarship.
4. If you don't apply, you can't qualify! I have counseled families before who didn't think they would qualify for money, but indeed they did! So please read on to find out more about the FAFSA.

What happens after the FAFSA is mailed or filed electronically?

After the FAFSA has been sent, it will take a few weeks to get a Student Aid Report (SAR). This confirms the information you entered on the FAFSA and it shows your EFC.

Besides asking several questions about the financial situation of the family, the FAFSA also asks for the colleges you are interested in attending. Your EFC information is sent to every college you listed on the FAFSA. Therefore, a few weeks after you receive the SAR, you will get an "award letter" from each college to which you applied which will outline how much money has been offered. For example an award letter may grant a student a $4,000 loan, a $2,000 grant and $2,500 in work-study. The family may accept any or all of the money. You will need to compare the award letters from each college. This may be the all-important factor in deciding where you will attend.

Also, remember to talk with college financial aid counselors if you have questions or if you need help filling out the FAFSA. It's their area of expertise and they enjoy helping students find ways of funding their college education.

Finally, you and your parents may understand financial aid better now (hopefully), but there must be just a little confusion jumbled in your brain. The following websites and timetable of financial aid events should help you.

www.fafsa.ed.gov
www.collegeboard.org
www.finaid.org

Financial Aid Timeline: Senior Year

Fall – Senior Year – Pick up a FAFSA from your guidance counselor, college counselor or financial aid office.

January – Parents, start thinking about filing taxes as soon as possible and then start filling out the FAFSA. The FAFSA may also be filed online at **www.fafsa.ed.gov**

March/April – These are the typical priority dates for all colleges for the FAFSA to be mailed or sent electronically. It will take approximately four to eight weeks to receive a *Student Aid Report* (SAR) back from the government and then you will receive your award letter stating how much money you have been awarded.

August/September – Financial aid money will be distributed to the student and/or put into the student's account.

You will need to re-file every year you are in college. Family circumstances may change; therefore your financial aid package will change. Every January, plan on re-applying for loans, grants and work-study.

Also, some students do not want their parent income to be considered because the student has been independent. A professional judgment committee in the financial aid department looks at situations such as these on an individual basis. Generally, parent income will be considered until the student is 24 years of age.

At the end of your college career, you will meet with financial aid counselors and participate in an exit counseling session. This will help you understand repayment options and plans.

Chapter Five

Scholarships
You Don't Have to be a Scholar

Topics Covered:

- **Different types of scholarships**
- **Scholarship search**
- **Scholarship scams**

Scholarships are awards of money given to a student for various reasons. The difference between a scholarship and financial aid money is that the student, by virtue of good grades, sports, or other achievements or talents, earns a scholarship. Here is a list of different types of scholarships:

Merit-Based Scholarship

A merit-based scholarship is based on grades.   The best resources for finding out more about merit-based scholarships are high school counselors, financial aid counselors and college admissions counselors.

Athletic Scholarship

An athletic scholarship is earned by being a top athlete. A college coach or recruiter may scout talented athletes to play for their college team. The best resources for finding out more about athletic scholarships are high school coaches, college admissions counselors, financial aid counselors, and college athletic departments.

Talent Scholarship

A talent scholarship can be earned through various talents such as debate, dance, music, and theater. College admissions counselors, high school counselors and heads of specific departments at colleges (dance, debate, theater, music, art) are great resources for these. Also, sometimes a high school teacher or drama coach will have information about particular scholarship awards.

First Generation College Scholarship

A first generation college scholarship is given to students who are first generation college students – in other words, in cases where neither parent received a college degree. Colleges have various guidelines for their first generation scholarship; ask a financial aid or college admissions counselor at the college you apply to if you think you may qualify.

Diversity Scholarship

Diversity scholarships are given to students who will contribute "diversity" to a college campus. Diversity means much more than ethnicity. You can contribute to the diversity of a campus by being a first generation college student, a member of a geographically under-represented area or being a female interested in the sciences or engineering fields. You should contact college admissions counselors, financial aid counselors, and diversity and equity offices on campus for information on these scholarships.

What other types of scholarships are there and where can I find out more?

Would you believe that some scholarships are never given away and the money isn't used because nobody applies? There are many organizations and companies you should research. Start with non-profit organizations and businesses in your local community. Use the scholarship search at the end of this chapter to help you find scholarships for which you may qualify. This is the time to ask all your relatives about organizations or clubs they may belong to; many companies and organizations have money allocated for scholarships for their employees or members. Also, community based or ethnically based organizations are great places to start your search.

Bottom line: Scholarships are not just for students who have high grades or are star athletes. Some scholarships require that you were raised in a single parent home, come from a particular state, have a learning disability, or that you have an ancestor from a particular background or profession. Do you see the possibilities here? Scholarship eligibility varies widely; chances are there is a scholarship out there for you!

When do I start researching scholarships?

You should start your research early, around your sophomore year in high school. I would recommend creating a folder and keeping deadlines and requirements in mind for particular scholarships. Many scholarship deadlines are actually in the last semester of your junior year. Remember, "Knowledge is power," so get to know what's out there and be prepared. You could apply for twenty scholarships, but only get three, but that's more than you would have had if you hadn't applied at all. And when it comes to paying the high costs of a college education, every little bit helps.

Some scholarships require that you answer specific questions on an application or write an essay on a selected topic. However, most scholarships simply ask that you write a general essay. In this case, the topic is up to you – for example, you could write about why you need the scholarship money, what it was like growing up in a single-parent home, how you would add diversity to a campus, how travel experiences or community service participation have impacted you, and so on.   Here's my recommendation: Write one general essay for all scholarship applications. You may apply for twenty, but you are only writing one essay. You're swamped with other tasks around you – work smarter, not harder.

Applying for scholarships while you are in college

Keep in mind that you may also apply for scholarships while you are attending college.   Scholarships are not just for entering freshmen.   Once you are in college you may apply for scholarships through the department of your major, continuing student scholarships through financial aid, clubs, sororities/fraternities or other organizations.   These scholarships may be based on a high grade point average in your major, or possibly a club in which you are active. Just because you don't get a scholarship as a freshman does not mean you cannot apply while you are in college.

Beware! Scholarship Scams

Unfortunately, there are scams out there that solicit and target anxious students and parents who want to apply for as many scholarships as possible. Be leery of any person or organization that claims they can get you scholarships. Generally speaking, if an organization is *charging* you to find scholarships, it's a scam. Use your resources and do your research. If you're not sure, ask a high school, college, or financial aid counselor. Some colleges may do a scholarship search for $20-$50; this is fine, but be wary of any individual or company who is asking for hundreds of dollars.

- Check out another free scholarship search website created in response to scams, **www.freschinfo.com**

- For information about fraudulent scholarship search scams check the Federal Trade Commission website at **www.ftc.gov**

Scholarship Checklist – Remember to start early! Sophomore year is not too soon.

First Generation College Student Scholarships

○ Did either of your parents get a college degree? If not, you are considered a *first generation college student* and there may be scholarship money for you.
○ Research at least ten colleges/universities regarding first generation college students. Look at their websites and talk with admissions and financial aid counselors.
○ Use the internet. (Hint: go to a search engine like **www.google.com** and type in "first generation college students.")
○ Create a file and record your findings.

Athletic Scholarships

- Talk with your coach about possibilities. Find out about guidelines/requirements/try-outs for athletic scholarships.
- Talk with your high school counselor about "Clearinghouse" guidelines for college athletics. Visit **www.ncaa.org/eligibility/cbsa/** for more information.
- Make contact with a college coach – research the college's website and make initial contact by phone or email with questions about being recruited for a sport.
- Create a file and record your findings.

Merit Scholarships

- Merit scholarships are based on exceptional grade point averages and ACT/SAT test scores.
- Look at least 20 colleges for merit scholarships. Research websites and make contact by email or phone with admission counselors and financial aid counselors.

o Make an appointment with your high school counselor and get information about at least ten merit scholarships offered through the high school and other scholarships in their scholarship file.

o Create a file and record your findings.

Talent Scholarships

o A talent scholarship may be earned in areas such as debate, dance, music and theater.

o Based on your talent, research at least 20 colleges with the department in which you are interested (dance, band, debate, etc). The best place to start is by talking to your teachers and coaches to find out which colleges have strong departments in your area of interest. Then, get on the internet and start your research.

o Using the internet, find at least ten talent scholarships. (Hint: use a search engine like **www.google.com** and type "dance scholarships.")

o Talk with your high school counselor about talent scholarships that may be offered through the high school.

o Create a file and record your findings.

Community Scholarships

- There are many organizations and companies within your local community that may offer scholarships.
- Research at least five non-profit or community organizations. Start with: Kiwanis, Rotary, Library, Elks, YMCA, and Chamber of Commerce.
- Ask at your church or synagogue about college scholarships offered through the religious institution you attend.
- Research at least 20 local businesses and corporations for scholarships. Start with: Wal Mart, Target, Taco Bell, McDonalds, Coca Cola, Girl Scouts, etc.
- Research at least ten product scholarships (e.g. Coca-Cola). Using the internet, look into scholarships from companies whose products you use and keep your eyes open for possibilities when shopping with mom or dad;, be aware of the back of cans and boxes that may have information.
- Ask your parents if their workplace or club offers scholarships to children of employees. This is very important and is often surprisingly under-used. Remember it never hurts to ask. Include aunts,

uncles, grandparents and other relatives in your
search also.

o   Create a file and record your findings.

Non-profits & Educational Opportunities

o   Research after-school programs and organizations
    that you may participate in during summer. Many of
    these programs offer not only college-prep
    workshops, but they also offer scholarships to their
    participants.

o   Use the glossary in the back of the book to do your
    own research to find scholarships and summer
    programs.

Be a Detective

o   Research and find at least 20 other scholarships.

o   Start by doing a free scholarship search at
    www.fastweb.com.

o   Go to **www.scholarshipexperts.com** and sign up for
    an e-newsletter.

- o Go to a bookstore or library or on-line and look up college magazines such as US News and World Report College Edition.
- o Using the internet and a search engine, type in words like; scholarships, first generation college student, learning disability scholarship, etc. and find your own resources.
- o Create a file and record your findings.

Good Luck with Your Scholarship Search!

Chapter Six

Gearing Up for the Transition from High School to College

Topics Covered:

- **What classes to take your senior year**
- **How to finish strong your senior year**

"Senioritis":   You're "sick" with the anticipation of finishing high school and you're ready to move on to college!

Let's face it: You have worked hard in high school and you are ready to start the next chapter of your life, pursuing your goals, meeting new people, going new places! High school was fun and it has prepared you to further your education and to be more independent. But you're a little nervous. Remember though, you are not the only one going to a new place, living in a new room with a person you have never met – *everyone* else is in the same situation as you. College is a different culture. Besides expanding your knowledge, college teaches you more about yourself as you make decisions on your own and make new friends.

You are about to venture on a journey that will be exciting, but don't forget about making a strong finish to your high school career! Are you contemplating taking easy classes to breeze through your senior year? Taking easy classes means getting better grades, which could help your admission to a college, right? Absolutely not! Admissions offices want to see a strong academic schedule as a sign that you are serious about your studies.

Focus on getting good grades your senior year, just as you have throughout your entire high school experience. Colleges can rescind (or reverse) their acceptance decision if they get your final grades (you will be required to send the college a final high school transcript), and you have failed classes. Some students have made the mistake of thinking that they could let their grades slip because they have already been accepted. Of course you wouldn't want to do anything to jeopardize acceptance to your top choice college.

Just remember to take challenging courses and do your best in those classes. By focusing on a strong high school finish, you will have a better chance of admission to the college of your choice, and you will be better prepared academically for college courses. Best of all, you'll finish your high school career knowing you made the most of it.

You have pondered the thought of college – how to prepare, how to pay and how to make the transition. You have made a good decision for yourself and your future. College graduates earn approximately $400 more per week than young adults with only a high school diploma. So stay on track, finish high school with a strong record and cruise into the college experience.

High school, especially your senior year, is a time in your life you will always remember. So make your last year a success – don't succumb to senior-itis. Accept the responsibility of being a leader in your high school. Do you remember when you were a freshman in high school? You looked up to the seniors. Be a good role model.   Give back by showing your school spirit, and enjoy being at the top of your school.   Before you know it, it will be graduation day and you will be a freshman again…in college!

Chapter Seven

Your First Semester of College
What to Expect and How to Prepare

Topics Covered:

- **Difference between high school & college classes**
- **Support services at colleges**

You are excited about going to college, being independent, having more freedom, making new friends, but let's face it, it's a big transition. You are also a little scared, nervous, and anxious. Just remember every new freshman is in the same situation as you – settling into the new dorm room, checking out the neighbors, wondering if they'll find their way to their first class.

Colleges understand this anticipation and stage of anxiety not only for students, but for parents as well, so they hold college orientation sessions the summer before classes begin. Orientation is just that, it helps students become "oriented" to their new surroundings, easing the tension, creating a comfort zone on the campus. Besides getting acquainted with the campus, the most intimidating event will probably be registering for classes. During registration, students meet with an academic advisor to discuss their goals, intended major, and which classes the student should take for the first semester.

College Classes vs. High School Classes

Most freshmen take 12-15 credits per semester or quarter. Before going any further, let's go back to the basics just for clarity. First, the term "credits" is another way to say "hours." Therefore, if a student is signed up for 15 credits, that student is taking 15 hours of classes per week.

The average class is three credits. Therefore, if a student is taking 15 credits, they are taking five classes. Usually, students must take at least 12 credits to be considered a full-time student and therefore be eligible for all financial aid, but check with your advisor to confirm this at your school. Your advisor will also help you plan a graduation date and establish how many credits you should take to graduate on time; most students need to take at least 15 credits per semester to graduate in four years.

Sometimes, overly zealous students want to register for more than 15 credits in the first semester/quarter; most advisors discourage this, especially while the student is getting adjusted to the difference between high school and college classes.

One difference you will love is that you can plan your own schedule. In high school you were used to going to class Monday through Friday from 8AM to 3PM. In college, you can arrange your own schedule. Generally, college classes are scheduled either on a Monday/Wednesday/Friday schedule or a Tuesday/Thursday schedule. Not only can you choose the days you want to go to class, you can also choose the times. In my case, since I had a part-time job as a tour guide in the afternoons, I chose classes in the morning. Also, I wanted Tuesdays and Thursdays free for studying, working, and enjoying everything college life had to offer. So my class schedule was usually Monday/Wednesday/Friday from 9AM-1PM.

Although college classes are typically more stimulating than high school classes, they are also more difficult. Professors will usually give you a syllabus on the first day of class that will list the textbooks you will need to buy, the upcoming test dates, assignment due dates, and reading assignments. You are expected to stay caught up on the reading; often there will be no reminder that the test is the next day or that the midterm paper is due next week.

Remember, most professors will have office hours in which you may ask questions, get help with an assignment or maybe just introduce yourself – I would actually encourage this if you are in a large class. By introducing yourself to the professor, you may be creating other opportunities for yourself. Perhaps he or she will remember you when he's looking for a teaching assistant or when the time comes to ask for a recommendation to graduate school.

There are so many things to think about; so many new adjustments to make. Although you may have looked forward to this new beginning and long-awaited independence, this can be a time of high stress and anxiety. Crossing the bridge from high school to college is one of the most important transitions you will make in your life. Students may become overwhelmed with their new obligations of studying, but also with personal struggles of making new friends, being homesick, and adapting to a new environment. College campuses are abundantly equipped with resources – tutoring, psychological counseling, career counseling and advising. Campuses offer support and a safe environment through advocacy offices for religious affiliations, gay and lesbian students, ethnic minorities and women.

As a student, I spent several hours at the career center taking personality tests and speaking to a counselor about my strengths, weaknesses, likes and dislikes regarding my career choices. I also took advantage of the tutoring services on campus not only to help me in a math class I struggled in, but also to keep up my grades in the English class I was doing well in. About half of the students who use the tutoring services are not students with low grades. In fact, these are some of the brightest students using their resources wisely to help them continue to have good study habits and consequently high grades.

Admissions offices are geared toward getting students into the college, but support services provide resources to the student throughout the duration of college. The goal is not only to admit students, but also to graduate students. The greater number of students who graduate, the better retention reputation the college will have, and that often brings more alumni donations as well as a more qualified applicant pool in the future. Remember the confusing question that was asked in the information session I attended when I was 18 – "What is the freshman retention rate?" This question addresses how many freshmen actually come back their sophomore year to continue their studies. A high freshman retention rate reveals a lot about the comfort of a college campus. If the retention rate is low, what does that say about the college?

Here is a list of support services provided on most college campuses:

- All religious affiliations (Christian, Jewish, Jehovah, Mormon, Buddhism, etc)

- Career counseling (personality testing and advising)
- Psychological counseling (depression, eating disorders, addiction)
- Health services
- Tutoring
- Ethnic minority/multicultural advocacy offices
- Women in engineering, math and science
- Women's resource center
- Gay and lesbian center

Chapter Eight

The Major Question
What Do You Want to Study?

Topics Covered:

- Do you have to choose a major your first year in college?
- How do you choose a major?
- A doctor's story

"If one advances confidently in the direction of his dreams and endeavors to live the life which he has imagined, he will meet with a success unexpected in common hours."

Henry David Thoreau

"What's your major?"

Get used to that question because it is going to come up a lot. From the time you are in high school through your college years, you will be asked this question by parents and peers. Given that more people who are well beyond their college years don't know what they want to do when they "grow up," how can it be expected that young adults just starting college will have the answer to that question? Although students should be thinking about their interests and what they want to study, it can put a lot of pressure on teenagers to choose a major when they are first starting college.

Let's look at a couple of scenarios.

1. Robert is a senior in high school and wants to major in biology because he wants to go to medical school. It's possible that Robert will excel in his college science classes and do well enough in college to apply to medical school. However, chances are higher that Robert will take gross anatomy (dissection of the human body) and faint at the first sight of the human cadavers. Robert may realize that

although the idea of being a doctor is appealing, his strength is not in the sciences. Or he may consider his weak stomach just a part of his learning and go on to be a great doctor!

2. Carlos is the first in his family to go to college. He wants to excel and take advantage of opportunities his parents did not have. Carlos wants to get a job that has high job security and a high starting salary so he decides to major in engineering. Students who graduate in this area are very marketable; job opportunity is wide and starting salaries are very appealing. Here's the problem: Carlos doesn't like computers; in fact, he hates math and science classes.

3. Laura wants to go to college because she knows that furthering her education will offer more job opportunity since most employers are seeking employees with at least a bachelor's degree. Laura is just starting her freshman year in college and she has a couple of ideas as to what she may want to study. She likes business, but she is also interested in psychology.   Actually, anthropology and

journalism sound intriguing as well. How will she figure out a major?

Do any of these sound familiar? The reality is that most college students do not know what they want to major in when they start college. The other reality is that those who think they do will change their major three to five times. Many students either have several ideas, like Laura in the previous example, or they don't have a clue what they want to study.

In my research and experience, I have learned that my best mentors had a difficult time deciding on their major, but pursued their passion and are now very successful. Whom do you look up to? What was their college experience like? Did she or he know exactly what they were going to major in when they started out? I challenge you to do a little research, maybe shadow someone in a career you're interested in; you may be surprised at the interesting things you will learn. I recently participated in "Take Our Daughters to Work," where a high school junior shadowed me for a couple of hours and we talked about being a writer. She said that she had always thought she wanted to be an author, but working with animals is also a passion of hers and that she had also considered being a veterinarian. I suggested writing about animals and combining the two interests; she liked that idea!

As I mentioned before, I have friends and mentors who are successful and happy in their careers, but did not find their path until a few years after their college graduation. Sometimes we need to have a little more life experience before we find our niche and true calling. I was recently at a writer's conference where I met a woman who earned a bachelor's degree in German, but worked in horticulture when she graduated, then moved into the computer industry and is now a writer and published author!

I have suggestions, remedies, and personal opinions about how a student comes to the decision of what they should study in college. First, I recommend to many of my students that they check off the "undecided" or "undeclared" box if a college application asks for their intended major.   Most four-year colleges require that students take two years of liberal arts courses in order to graduate.

This means that a student can actually be "undecided" as to a major until the end of his or her sophomore year.

Why is this beneficial? Being "undeclared" allows a student to experiment with different classes, "test the waters," and find what piques their interest. So, let's say, in an introductory psychology class you realize you love studying psychology and the human mind. You also realize you are struggling with a chemistry course and you dread going to every class. Through trial and error, you are learning what you like and dislike, and maybe you will decide to major in psychology.

Young adults go through many changes while they are in college. They are learning more about themselves and their strengths and weaknesses. Perhaps the person you were when you first started applying to college when you wanted to major in pre-law has now developed into a "truer" self and you've matured and found a love for engineering. It's not an uncommon story.

Finally, when you get to college, meet new people, learn new things, you will find out about areas of study you didn't even know existed. You may decide to explore other options, ones you had never before considered.

Unfortunately I often consult with students who are persuaded by their parents to choose one particular major, perhaps because of job security, high starting salaries or an expectation that the student will enter the family business. I try to get these students to focus on finding what truly interests them and to choose an area of study they will enjoy.

If you study a subject you love, chances are it is going to lead to success for you. Some students tell me they couldn't possibly major in sociology because there aren't as many jobs as there are for engineering majors. They have the equation backwards; *it is what you make of your college experience that builds your resume.* The truth is that only about three out of ten people are actually working in the field in which they majored in college. Try this: Fill in the blank below:

If money were not an issue, I would major in

_____.

The true value of going to college comes not only from the classroom, but also from the total learning experience. Obviously, there are some things to consider if you're interested in graduate school or doctoral study. For example, if you are interested in medical school, you will be required to take specific classes such as organic chemistry and calculus when you are an undergraduate – these classes are called prerequisites. You would have to take these classes before applying to medical school.

So there are some boundaries of what you **should** study versus what you **would** like to study. However, generally speaking, I recommend to the students who consult with me to first think about an "undeclared" or "undecided" major in order to give him or her more time to explore different interests. Then, I encourage them to major in what interests <u>them</u> and what they have a passion for, not what mom and dad want them to study or what they assume will earn them a high starting salary.

All of this is not to say that if a student chooses a major, let's say architecture for example, that they will not be able to change it if they realize they have trouble building a toothpick bridge. Changing your major is a part of the college experience; I know, I did it three times!

It is quite amazing how events happen for a reason. I started as an occupational therapy major, but did an internship in that field and realized it was not for me. I was encouraged to pursue it because all the career tests I took said that I should be in a "helping profession" and occupational therapy fit that category. People would say, "Oh, you're such a compassionate person and you'll be a great occupational therapist." Yet, during my internship I realized that one of my weaknesses is impatience, which is not a good trait for an occupational therapist. That was lesson number one.

Then I thought majoring in business would be a good move; employers were hiring business majors, offering good starting salaries, and yes, there were some aspects of business I liked. But I quickly learned that business was too analytical for me (not to mention I received a D in accounting -- the only D I ever received!)

So I went marching into the career center again, researching different careers. I am not saying that career assessment tests are not helpful, because they are; in fact it's a good place to start. However, as we will discuss in the next chapter, it's your college experiences that will pave your path to your true passion and interest.

My friend Kristin told me about studying liberal arts and how it provided a well-rounded education. So I tried it out and loved it! That was my final major – liberal arts with a concentration in psychology. Once I made this decision I began to enjoy my classes so much more. I was so relieved; I found out later that about 60% of liberal arts graduates become CEOs!

Whether you are a senior in high school thinking about a major or a sophomore in college who cannot decide on a major, you are no doubt stressed about it. You feel like everyone else knows what he or she wants to study. You feel like time is working against you; after all, you're a sophomore in college, how could you not know what you want to study? Trust me, this is normal and you are not the only student who feels this pressure.

Peers, advisors, professors, parents, all will have their input saying, "Oh, I knew someone who graduated with that degree and they couldn't find a job." You will hear a lot of "wisdom" like this and while it's good to get advice, don't let others make your decision for you. As you will read in the next chapter, there are many things you can do in college to help you decide on your major, but above all find something you are passionate about and truly interested in studying. You will also be assigned an advisor that will guide and counsel you toward a major that is right for your strengths and interests.

A Doctor's Story

At first glance, Dr. Smith's story seems almost fairytale – he's smart, did well on his SATs and is now a successful surgeon. But what makes him such a phenomenal doctor, one who relates so well with his patients, is his character, which comes from his life experiences. Dr. Smith grew up on a farm in a small town in Texas. He remembers being inspired as a child by a doctor in a near-by town (his town did not have any doctors). He was one of few in his class who went to college and he was a first generation, low-income college student. He actually took the SATs four times and did well on math, but never improved on English.

Indeed, Dr. Smith is successful because he studied a lot, but like many of the first generation college students I work with, he said he just persisted through college and learned by trial and lots of errors. Also, like many first gens, he describes his family as "strong, silent supporters," always encouraging him and telling him that he could do anything.

If you're thinking about becoming a medical doctor, Dr. Smith recommends talking with physicians to get their perspective on what it took to get where they are. Knowing what is involved in the training can be very helpful in planning the future and deciding if medicine is right for you.

As a young adult entering college, you also have a story to tell - facts such as - where you're from, what your aspirations are and why. But also, as you go along your path, your life experiences will make your narrative more interesting. What is your story? What do you imagine it to be in 10 or 20 years?   As you think about this or even write it down (this info makes a great admissions essay), remember that you are the author of your story, but life makes a great editor.

Chapter Nine

Making Your College Years Count

Topics Covered:

- **College is more than studying**
- **Sports in college**
- **Studying in a different country**
- **Working on campus & internships**

"I never let my schooling interfere with my education."

Mark Twain

Here's the real college tip, the real scoop: Research shows approximately 60% of what you learn and retain in college comes from outside of the classroom. Obviously, you are going to college to learn academics and you will; professors who have been in their fields of study for many years will enrich you. You will find the lectures in college to be stimulating -- more in depth and more challenging than in high school. With the exception of a few professors who are less than exciting, you may find the academic environment a bit overwhelming, but that's part of the learning process too.

You will get to choose your own classes and create your own schedules. In most high schools, the curriculum is straightforward, but in college you can choose from courses such as "Anthropology and Forensics of the Human Body" to the "Psychology of Deviant Behavior" to "Underwater Basket Weaving." Okay, maybe not basket weaving, but you get the idea.

College is so much more than academics; it is a way of life. Once you leave the classroom, you are still learning. You are meeting new people, getting adjusted to your dorm situation, working towards independence. Your new life *is* a classroom. *The key is to be a balanced student.* That means doing well in your courses, but getting involved in campus and community activities too. Before I give you ideas of things you can and should do while you are in college, allow me to explain why being a balanced, well-rounded student is so critical to your future career and for that matter, your future life.

If you were an employer, would you rather hire someone who had received straight A's in college, or someone who had an average college grade point average, but was involved with organizations on campus and took an active role in student government? The answer is easy, or at least it should be – an employer wants to hire an employee who is well-rounded.

Getting straight A's is commendable and I encourage students to strive for high grades, but remember every experience in college is a learning experience. So if you received a C in molecular biology, but in the process you learned better study habits by asking the professor for extra help or became more disciplined about your time, you learned where your weaknesses were and got something out of the experiences.

<u>College is more than studying; it's all about learning</u>

So, to repeat, studying and getting good grades is definitely a priority, but it is not *everything*. Getting involved while you are in college will help you determine what your strengths and weaknesses, likes and dislikes and passions are.

So what does "involved" mean? Let's start with clubs and organizations; every college has them, some larger universities have as many as 400 clubs! There is truly a club for every possible interest on campus. So let's say you are a political science major; you may want to get involved in student government and run for an office. Or maybe you are studying psychology and you think it would be beneficial (and fun) to know sign language. Maybe you're from Texas, but you wanted to go to college in Colorado so you could spend time enjoying your true passion – snowboarding! Whatever your interest, there is sure to be a club on campus for you, and if there isn't, you can always start one!

Depending on the college, fraternities and sororities can make up a big part of the social life on campus. Greek organizations may or may not be something you want to be involved in, but in the first weeks of the semester, fraternities and sororities will be "rushing" for new members. Whether you join a club, fraternity or sorority, each one can provide a smaller group in an overwhelming social scene, especially at a larger university.

<u>Sports</u>

Most colleges have club or intramural sports. Besides having fun and getting to know people by participating in sports, you are also getting exercise – a great stress reducer during finals week! College students undergo many changes: moving away from home, becoming independent, meeting new people, studying, studying, and studying -- it's important to remember to take care of yourself mentally and physically. Joining the water polo team or the ski team is sure to reduce your stress.

Sports and recreation are another great aspect of college. In your college fees, you are charged for the Recreation Center and all of the amenities (whether you like it or not). Notice the environment and community around you. Is there skiing, surfing, biking, hiking? What activities are accessible to you so you can let off some steam after cramming for that philosophy exam?

Study Abroad

Studying abroad is a great way to add travel and culture to your college experience. Most colleges offer a wide variety of study abroad programs. You may want to study in Europe for a semester, maybe a year or quite possibly just a couple of weeks in the summer. Expand your horizons by studying in places like Australia, Mexico, Ireland, just about anywhere in the world! Some colleges even offer a "semester at sea" program where a student can study on a ship for a semester.

A study abroad program may seem ideal for a Spanish major wanting to study in Argentina, but it's also a great experience (and one employers love to see on a resume) no matter what your major. Most students go abroad the beginning of their junior year in college. Check with the college study abroad office for more details on places to study and when the best time would be to fit this into your college schedule.

Many students do not even consider studying abroad because they think it will be too expensive. Actually, most colleges have reciprocal agreements with other international schools so the cost can be the just the same. Also, there are often scholarships available for study abroad. Start your research your freshman or sophomore year in college, and again, be sure to visit with a study abroad counselor.

Work-study and Internships

Should you get a job while you are in college? Is work considered an extracurricular activity? Absolutely! I encourage students to work while they are in college, although perhaps not the first semester while you're making so many other adjustments. Studies show that students who have a part-time job manage their time better and actually get better grades. Not to mention the fact that job experience looks great on a resume. Besides, the extra cash will always come in handy! But make sure you haven't over-programmed yourself with classes and other activities before you make a commitment to a job.

If you feel you can handle a part-time job, carefully consider your options. Use the resources around you. In chapter four I talked about how beneficial work-study can be; think about what departments on campus are related to your major. Here's a tip: if you know or learn of a department or organization that fits your major and you think it would be great job experience, take initiative. Do not wait for job listings to come out in the campus paper a week before classes start. Call them – actually, even better, go to the offices and approach them the summer before you start college.

By getting involved in other aspects of college, whether it is a part-time job or a club, you are getting more out of your college experience and building a resume and future references at the same time. Networking is crucial. You have probably heard the phrase, "It's not what you know, but who you know." This is often true and it helps to have references to make those connections. Networking is a valuable tool that will not only help you in college, but can also pave a path for your career.

Create a Place to Call Home

You will be in college for at least four years. Establishing a community that is comfortable, inviting and home-like will make your years in college much more enjoyable. Getting involved will also allow you to make new friends. It's scary when you first get to college; suddenly you're a freshman again and you may feel a bit nervous about all the changes in your life. Developing good friendships will make you feel like you belong and will make you a happier, more successful student.

Students seem to be getting smarter and admission to college is getting more competitive. Today's job market is much the same. In the past, people who had a college degree could find a good job and make their way up the corporate ladder. Today, there's much more competition. Recent college graduates bring much more to the table than just a degree. They are creative, innovative, experienced through involvement, research, hands-on projects, internships and work-study. Use the *Notes* page to make a list of things you can do and people you can connect with in order to network and start building your resume.

Chapter Ten

Don't Forget to Enjoy the Ride – College Express!

Topics Covered:

- **College goes by fast; don't miss the opportunities!**
- **Take advantage of the activities going on!**

You are in college to study, to broaden your horizons, to prepare yourself for the future. However, although doing well in your classes is your priority, it's important to remember to enjoy this life experience. When you were a little kid, it seemed time moved so slowly. ("Are we there yet?" "When is Santa coming?" "How many more days until my birthday?") Time just couldn't go by fast enough.

I've learned that the older I get, the faster time seems to go by – now I want it to slow down! My point is that high school probably went by pretty fast for you; I promise you that college will go by even faster.

When I first arrived on campus as a freshman and looked around with awe, I felt excited and independent and I thought, "I never want to leave college, this place is great!" However, after four years, believe it or not, I was ready to graduate and move on to the next phase of my life.

So here's what to expect: You will arrive on campus, move into your dorm, and start meeting people. You'll go to amazing lectures, classes that get you excited about learning; you'll go to football games and weekend excursions with friends. The friends you make in college will most likely be your friends for life.

A college campus is a whole other world. Many people choose to work on a college campus after they graduate because of the energy and ideas that surround them. There's a reason you or your parents are paying that high tuition – take a look around the campus; there is a lot going on: research, plays, concerts, sports, cultural events. It's challenging and exciting!

You may have noticed parents on a college tour who are "reliving" their own college experience. They'll say, "I remember when..." and they'll tell a story about when they were in college. When I was a tour guide in college, I often met parents who would say, when describing their own college experience, that it all went by very fast, and they're right! So take advantage of being young, realize your potential and take the time to enjoy the thrills of being a college student.

When you were younger, you probably said, "When I grow up..." It's that time in your life; you've grown up! You are starting to make adult decisions and taking the steps to accomplish your goals. Restate your goals and dreams, write them down, and make your vision of a balanced college experience a reality.

Chapter Eleven

Community Colleges & the Option of Transferring

Topics Covered:

- **Starting at a community college and transferring to a 4-year college**
- **What are your options as a transfer student?**

Many students I work with ask whether or not they should attend a two-year school. There are many positive reasons for attending a two-year college and then transferring to a four-year college or university. First, let's talk about the difference between a community college (two years) and a college or university (four years).

Earning an Associate's Degree

Many students attend a community college to obtain an associate's degree and then go out to the work force. The pros of an associate's degree are:

1. Any education after high school is going to benefit you.
2. If your passion for a career requires only an associate's degree then you can start your life's work sooner.
3. If you *do* decide to further your education ten, even twenty years later, you can still do that.

The flip side of getting an associate's degree is that many employers still seek employees with at least a bachelor's degree. Therefore, job opportunities in some fields may be more limited with an associate's degree. The answer lies within your needs, interests and passion for what you want to do in life and in your career.

Starting at a Community College and Transferring to a Four-Year School

Should you start small (community college) and work your way into a larger university? Again, this depends upon your needs.

There are many reasons a student might begin at a community college and then transfer.

1. Often, a student's education funds are limited, and she may not be able to afford the cost of a large university. She may plan to go to a community college for two years and then transfer. Community colleges have less expensive tuition and fees, and can save her a few thousand dollars.

2. Maybe a student is from a small high school and may not be ready for a university of twenty thousand students and classes of three hundred or more in a lecture hall. The idea is to start small and work your way up. I graduated with a senior class of forty-five students. When I went to a large university and had a biology class of four hundred students, it was a bit of a culture shock. However, I had lived in a small town all of my life, where everyone knew me. I wanted to attend a large university and I adjusted well. It depends on your individual needs and wants.

3. Perhaps a student's grades in high school are not high enough to get into a university, so he needs to attend a

community college first, establish a good GPA and then transfer to a university. Most universities have minimum standards for grades and test scores. If you do not meet them, you may not get accepted. Community colleges, on the other hand, offer open enrollment, which means that they have no minimums – anyone can attend.

Here's a tip: Most four-year schools will consider you a *transfer*, not a *freshman* if you have college credit from another school such as a community college. Then, the university will look at the GPA you have earned at the community college, and often will not consider your high school grades. They may even waive the requirement of an ACT or SAT score.

Your job is to talk to someone at the University of your choice and to find out how many credits you need to earn at the community college to be considered a transfer student. Here's another tip: If you were a student with low grades in high school, you may start with a clean slate at a community college as you establish a new and improved college GPA. However, your college grades, in most cases, will always be considered.

The bottom line is, it does not matter where you *start*, but where you *finish*. The ultimate goal is the degree. I believe a student can have a more traditional college experience if they attend a four-year school – enjoying a traditional college campus life, living in a dorm, going to sporting events, but the question is – where are you going to be successful?

Use the *Notes* page in the back of the book to make a list of your needs/wants/desires in your ideal college environment. Look at lots of campus web sites and catalogs to see what "speaks" to you. If you can visit a campus, great! If you do visit, try to spend a night in the dorms. All colleges will help you arrange this and it's a great way to see if that campus feels like a good "fit." Also, be sure to let the admissions folks know (maybe in your interview or application essay) that you've visited the campus. Student interest is becoming a very important factor in admissions these days. But don't worry if you can't get to a campus you're interested in; admissions counselors know it's not always possible.

The Transfer Process

I know what you're thinking – how can I start at a two-year school and then transfer to a four-year school? That's two years at a community college and then two years at a four-year school and you will have your bachelor's degree. This sounds confusing; I know, read the last sentence again and then read on about transferring.

Let's look at an example.

Scenario A: Liz wants to study computer science. If she goes to a community college, studies for two years, and gets an associate's degree, most of what she will be studying is computer science.

Scenario B: If Liz decides to go to a university, a four-year school, she will not only study computer science, but history, speech, composition, psychology and a wide variety of other classes, otherwise known as *general academic courses*.

So why would you want to take history or speech if your major is computer science? You may not, but it will make you a more well rounded person and a marketable employee. Your degree will be computer science and you will be an expert in that field, but you will also know a little something about writing, art, public speaking, psychology, history, etc.

If you decide to transfer, you will take the general academic core classes at a community college and then transfer those classes to a four-year college. Chances are you can start taking classes in your major when you start your third year in college.

Do you see the difference? If you are confused by the terminology, remember to refer to the glossary in the back of the book. Be sure to ask your college counselor about transfer agreements between community colleges and the university you would like to attend. This is very important: Make sure your credits will transfer BEFORE signing up for a class.

So, to re-cap, here are your options regarding a community college or a university:

Option A: Attend a community college and earn an associate's degree (two years), then start your career.

Option B: Attend a university/college (four years) and earn a bachelor's degree.

Option C: Combination – start at a community college, then transfer to a four-year institution and finish with a bachelor's degree.

Many times a student will attend a community college because he or she is interested in vocational careers such as dental hygiene, auto mechanics or cosmetology. Make a list of potential careers that interest you. What would be a better fit for your goals – an associate's degree or a bachelor's degree?

Chapter Twelve

A Special Section for Parents

Topics Covered:

- **What to do when your student calls home**
- **How to support your college student**

"Selfhood begins with a walking way and love is proved in the letting go."

C. Lewis

Admit it, as parents; this is a hectic, anxious time for you as well. Whether you are excited about having the alone time you and your husband have dreamed about for years, or you're anticipating "empty nest" syndrome, it is understandable that you may be a little nervous about the college process.

After going through all the school years and then the college admissions process, parents often feel a real letdown once their child leaves home. Many parents have a difficult time with a quiet house and sometimes don't know what to do with their free time. Perhaps this is your last son or daughter to leave home, and there are now fewer demands for rides, meals, etc. If you suddenly find you are not "soccer mom" anymore, and you are not waiting up late nights to make sure that a curfew is met, it's a big change in your life! Being a teenager is tough, but being the parent of a teenager also brings challenges. The flip side is true; being in high school is one of the best times in a student's growth, but as parents you have been able to enjoy the last four years, too. You were there for try-outs, crushes, preparation for prom, watching your teen play sports or participate in a play and you were their number one fan. So it is understandable that you are now dealing with this transition from high school to college.

Some of you may be thinking right now, "Are you kidding – I can't wait for the day when I have more "me" time!" Nevertheless, after having a child at home for 18 years or so, it's often hard to let go, especially if it is your youngest child. And if you still have other children at home, be prepared for a big change in the family dynamics. It takes a while for all the family members to adjust to one less person in the house.

I encourage you to support your new college student in this stage of transition, by learning to say "No." That's right, "No." Students often get to college and call home wanting to know what to do about the roommate they hate or the class they're having trouble with. It's important to listen, perhaps give some advice, but then encourage them to seek the resources to figure it out themselves. This will help your children to become independent. I know it will be hard; you can hear the anxiety in their voice and as parents you want to fix it, but try to control the urge. Students are going to learn a lot from making mistakes and actually learning life's lessons. Of course, you should absolutely intervene if you feel there is any possible danger to your child or any other student.

Your first visit to see your son or daughter will probably be Parents' Weekend, which is usually in September or October. Then you can see how well they are doing and you can meet their new friends. Seeing your son or daughter's new independence should ease your mind and make you proud that you helped get them where they are!

A mom told me this story about visiting her daughter who was a freshman in college. They were planning a day of exploring the campus together and meeting her daughter's new friends. Her daughter was very excited about her dorm room – the place she would call home for at least a year. It was small, but was decorated trendy and fun and filled with all of the college essentials – books, computer, mini-fridge, posters, and other details that made it very eclectic. Mom noticed, on the bulletin board, a picture of three midriffs, all of which had navel rings. Yep, you guessed it – one of those bare bellies happened to be her daughter's! After mom's initial shock, she realized that her daughter was an adult and saw from her new lifestyle that overall she was living and studying very responsibly. After much thought, mom realized she would pick her battles and this would not be one of them (of course not before the "mom" talk about not piercing parts of your body that should not be pierced!)

Here is another tip for parents – students love mail, especially "care" packages! A feeling of homesickness can be easily cured with a package of homemade goodies mailed from mom! When I first got to college, my mom periodically sent me packages filled with chocolate treats, microwave popcorn, a CD or two, stationery and candles. Surprises like that always made my day and made my dorm room feel a little more like home.

After the first semester is over, you will start getting used to the idea that your son or daughter is making the transition into adulthood, and you can look forward to their coming home for the holidays – with all of their laundry and maybe a tattoo!

Glossary

This section of the book is simply to give you straightforward, easy definitions of college jargon. Whether you're reading a college viewbook, listening to an admissions or financial aid presentation, or taking a tour, you will undoubtedly be bombarded by new college lingo. Please make use of the section; use it as a resource as you explore your college options. To make the explanations easier to understand, I have used sample scenarios whenever possible.

Associate's Degree – A two-year degree earned through a community or junior college. See the definitions for bachelor's, master's, and doctorate degrees.

Bachelor's Degree – A four-year degree earned through a college or university. A bachelor's degree is the same as undergraduate degree. See definitions for graduate degree, associate's, master's and doctorate degrees to compare differences.

Credits – "Credits" means the same as "hours". Credit/hours is the number of classes you are taking in a semester. Example: Most classes are 3 credits, therefore, if a student is taking 15 credits (or 15 hours), they are taking 5 classes. As a general rule, most colleges encourage freshman to take between 12-15 (4-5 classes) credits their first semester and usually a student must have at least 12 credits to be considered a full-time study (which is often required many times for financial aid). Also, taking less than 12 credits a semester is going to cause the student to be in school longer than 4 years. Do you see how all of this is connected?

Doctorate Degree – Also known as a Ph.D., a doctorate degree is the highest degree a student can obtain. It usually takes at least an additional four years after a bachelor's degree is completed. See definition for associate's, bachelor's, master's, graduate, and undergraduate for clarification and comparison.

First Generation College Student – A student is considered a first generation college student if neither parent received a college degree.

If either or both of your parents started college but did not finish, you are still considered a first generation. If there is an older sibling who went to college, you are still considered first generation, because again, it's your parents who did not earn a degree.

Four-Year Graduation Rate – This is the percentage of students who graduate from college in four years. Allow me to explain a little further: the national average (all colleges in the U.S.) freshman graduation rate is about 34% which seems low: Only 34% of students are graduating in four years!? There are often good reasons for this. For example, many students don't graduate in four years because they studied abroad and weren't able to get all of their required classes in (although with careful planning, this may never be a problem). Some students may be doing a five-year bachelor's/master's degree combination program, which in fact will save time (and money), in the long run. Sometimes there is an inability to get into classes because they are full, which may result in having to stay an extra semester. (This often happens at large state universities, but almost never in smaller colleges.) So the next question is "What percentage of students graduate in five years?" Chances are it will be much higher than the four-year graduation rate. When asking about the four-year graduation rate, students and parents really want to know if it is taking students much longer to graduate because more time means more tuition money.

Freshman Retention Rate – This refers to the percentage of students who return for the second year of college. This statistic will give you a good idea of how many freshman students liked their first year experience and actually came back. For example, an 83% freshman retention rate would mean that 83% of the freshman students came back for their second year of college. A retention rate that high is a sign of a happy, successful student population.

Graduate degree/Graduate school – A graduate degree is a master's degree, either in science or the liberal arts. It's a degree obtained after a bachelor's degree. A graduate degree usually takes two additional years beyond your bachelor's degree. See definitions for associate's, bachelor's, master's, undergraduate and doctorate degrees for clarification and comparison.

Major – This is a student's main area of interest, or what they are studying in college. For example, my major in college was psychology. Your major may be engineering or business. Many students choose to "double major," earning enough credits in two departments to qualify for this dual degree.

Master's Degree – Same as a graduate degree – a master's degree is obtained after a bachelor's and usually takes at least two more years after your bachelor's degree is earned.

Minor – A minor may or may not be in the field that the student has a major in. A minor may complement a major or could be in a completely different area of study. For example, business majors may find it useful to minor in Spanish. Business and Spanish complement one another. On the other hand, a pre-med student may major in biology, but minor in music. Minors are typically 21-25 credits or 7-8 classes.

Prerequisite – A prerequisite is a class that must be taken before another class can be taken. For example, General Chemistry is a prerequisite for Organic Chemistry.

Rolling Admissions Process - This refers to how and when applications are reviewed and decided. Basically "rolling" means that applications are continually reviewed and decided. In these cases, a decision letter is mailed approximately four to eight weeks after the application is received. Most colleges do not having rolling admissions however, and send their letters out in late March or early April. If it's an acceptance, the school usually asks that the student confirm their desire to attend and reserve their spot by mailing back a deposit by May 1. Between the time that acceptance letters are mailed out and that May 1 deadline, many private schools hold what they call "prospective" weekends. These are geared toward trying to convince those students they have accepted into accepting *them*. If the student is able to visit the campus at this time, it's a good chance to ask any last minute questions before deciding if that school is a good fit.

Student to Faculty Ratio – This is the number of students there are for every professor. For example, a 15 to1 student/faculty ratio is 15 students for every 1 professor.

Suitcase Campus – This term is used to describe a campus where students tend to go home (or elsewhere) every weekend because there's not much to do on the campus. "Suitcase" campus portrays a negative college atmosphere where students "pack their suitcases" so to speak, every weekend to go somewhere else for social activities.

Undecided Major – Undecided is also known as Open Option or Undeclared and simply means the student has not decided on a major. Many freshmen think they have to choose a major because they are going to college. In reality, they can start college undecided and choose a major later, usually at the end of their sophomore year in college.

Viewbook – This is a booklet or pamphlet which gives a general overview of the college. You should pick up a viewbook from every college you're interested in; the viewbooks are available at college fairs, high school counselors, or college admissions offices.

Websites

www.act.org	ACT Test information and test dates
www.collegeboard.org	SAT Test information, test dates
www.usnews.com	"Best Colleges" Ranking
www.petersons.com	Admissions and Financial Aid
www.nacac.com	Admissions information
www.collegeboard.org	Practice EFC Calculation
www.finaid.org	Financial Aid Information
www.fafsa.ed.gov	File FAFSA electronically
www.fastweb.com	Free Scholarship Search
www.freschinfo.com	Scholarship Scam Information
www.ftc.com	Scholarship Scam Information

The use of the internet is becoming a necessary tool for research and finding more up-to-date resources in a shorter amount of time. Colleges are following the trend; students cannot only find out more about a college online, but also apply for admission, apply for financial aid and scholarships, schedule campus visits and register for classes.

When searching for information on a particular college or if you're doing a scholarship search, simply type in key words such as the name of the college and terms like: college, scholarships, financial aid, first generation college students, learning disabilities scholarship, diversity scholarship and so on. Record any useful websites you find on this page.

Other Websites:

A Resource for Students and Educators

Organizations that Support & Motivate First Generation College Students

AVID Center
www.avidonline.org

California Student Opportunity & Access Program (Cal SOAP)
www.sbcalsoap.org

College Summit Inc.
www.collegesummit.org

The Daniels College Prep & Scholarship Program
www.danielsfund.org

Gear Up: Gaining early awareness and readiness for undergraduate programs
www.ed.gov/gearup

Heart of Los Angeles (HOLA)
www.heartofla.org

Low-Income Families' Empowerment Through Education (Lifetime)
www.geds-to-phds.org

Magic Johnson Foundation
www.magicjohnson.org

Posse Foundation
www.possefoundation.org

**Organizations that Support & Motivate First Generation College Students
cont'd**

INROADS, Inc.
www.inroads.org

The Puente Project
www.puenteproject.org

EOPS: Extended Opportunity Programs and Services
California Community Colleges

Federal Trio Programs
www.ed.gov

Notes

Notes cont'd

Goals

_____

_____

_____

_____

_____

_____

_____

_____

_____

_____

_____

_____

_____

_____

_____

_____

Contacts/Resources/References

About the Author

I was a first generation college student and attended a small high school in Southern Colorado. At the time, my high school had about 200 students and my graduating class was 45 students. Needless to say, it was a bit of a culture shock when I arrived at Colorado State University, which had a student population of 23,000 at the time. A big university was exactly what I was yearning for; having grown up in a small town on a ranch, I was ready for more.

Through my personal, educational and professional experiences in working with young adults, I saw a need for first generation college students to get more guidance through the college admissions process. I dreamed of writing this book, but found myself getting caught up in the "real world" and not having the time or energy to follow through with my goal. At the age of 25 I decided to take a leap of faith. I left my job, sold everything I owned, and moved to the place I had always dreamed of living – Santa Barbara, California.

In May of 2004, I completed my master's degree in college student affairs from Azusa Pacific University. At APU, I got a different, but extremely insightful, perspective of college students. I led the efforts to start the first women's resource center at a California Christian college. This was a real educational experience for me and paved the way for my future work with organizations like Girls Inc.

My hope is that this book will bring information and motivation to students who want to pursue their college dreams and subsequently set an example for their own children. It is for anyone who feels intimidated by the process of applying to or going to college – believe me, if I can do it, so can you! I hope we can ultimately bring more diversity to our college campuses by supporting students who need a little nudge and a little extra inspiration. I pray that young adults learn how to realize their potential and ambitions and use college as a stepping-stone to learn more about themselves and the life they want to live.

If you have a question or would like to share your college story or how the book has helped you, please visit **www.advocacypress.com**. I look forward to hearing from you and allowing you to help me make this information current, vibrant and accessible.

About the Cover Designer

Lora Tomova was born and raised in Bulgaria, and moved to the U.S. when she graduated from high school. She lived in New York for a while, trying to decide what she wanted to study in college. When she discovered graphic design it was clear that she had found her passion. She relates to the problems encountered by first generation college students because she found it very difficult herself to fill out a college application in a language other than her own. Lora is currently completing her BFA in Graphic Design at the Academy of Art in San Francisco and beginning her career as a designer.

About the Editor

Ronna Gordon is a former teacher, textbook editor, and contributing writer, and currently works as an educational consultant in Santa Barbara, California. She can be reached at **www.ronnagordon.com**.